GW00361652

DREAMS

AND

SUDDEN DANGERS

To Elaine

With best wishes

Tony 26/3/2011

Also by Tony Turner

Some I Did Earlier (TWM Publishing, 1996)

Reading The Signs (Cherrycroft Press, 1998)

Where Was I? (Cherrycroft Press, 2000)

Belief in Something Better (Cherrycroft Press, 2003)

How Far Away Australia Is (Cherrycroft Press, 2005)

Oxford, 1953-57 (Cherrycroft Press, 2007)

TONY TURNER was born in Rabaul, New Guinea, in 1933 and grew up there and in Hong Kong, Manila, Sydney, Nottingham, Sheffield, Kingston-on-Thames and Ealing. He was educated at Cranbrook School (Sydney), Allhallows School (Devon) and Keble College (Oxford). Apart from two years at Their Majesties' pleasure in the Royal Engineers, he spent his official working life in ICI as an industrial chemist. He lives in Cookham, Berkshire and has a wife, two sons and a daughter, five grandchildren and not enough time.

He started to write poems during his Devon schooldays and continued to write intermittently while earning a living and bringing up a family. Theoretically retiring in 1990, he has been writing regularly ever since. His poems have been published widely in poetry magazines and anthologies and he has five previous collections: *Some I Did Earlier* (1996), *Reading The Signs* (1998), *Where Was I?* (2000), *Belief In Something Better* (2003), *How Far Away Australia Is* (2005) in addition to the autobiographical poem sequence, *Oxford 1953-57* (2007)

He enjoys sharing poetry with others in Metroland and Temys Poets and giving readings, which he has done in venues all over the south from Hitchin to Penzance.

Tony Turner

DREAMS

AND

SUDDEN DANGERS

Published in the UK by
Cherrycroft Press
Popes Lane
Cookham Dean
Berks
SL6 9NY

Produced by
Manuscript Research
P.O. Box 33, Bicester, OX26 4ZZ
Tel: 01869 323447
Printed and bound by
MWL Print Group, S. Wales

Poems © Tony Turner, 2009

Cover design © Tony Turner, 2009

All rights reserved. No part of this publication may be
reproduced, stored in a retrieval system, rebound or
transmitted in any form or by any means, electronic,
mechanical, photocopying, scanning, recording or otherwise
without the prior written permission of the author, nor be
otherwise circulated in any form of binding or cover other
than that in which it is published without a similar condition
being imposed on the subsequent purchaser.

British Library cataloguing in Publication Data. A catalogue
record for this book is available from the British Library.

ISBN   978-0-9532900-9-3

ACKNOWLEDGEMENTS

Thanks to Frances Wilson for editorial advice concerning
this and all my other collections.

Thanks also to the editors of the following periodicals in
whose pages some of these poems first appeared:

*Acumen, The Interpreter's House, Iota, Pennine Platform,
Poetry Cornwall, Poetry Nottingham, Quadrant (Australia),
Quattrocento, Rhyme & Reason* and *South.*

For all those who send messages in bottles

CONTENTS

NOTICE

This poem has been deactivated
to prevent infringement of copyright.
Some essential words have been removed
to disable the poem, make it unsuitable
for reading, declaiming, reprinting, defaming,
reviewing, renewing, revising, undoing,
analysing, reprising, learning by heart,
taking apart, or any other purpose
whether oral, moral, immoral
mechanical, electronic, evangelical or moronic
without prior written permission
and the payment of a small commission
to me, my agent, publisher, lover
or some other approved and accredited person.

DREAMS

I dreamt I was a genius
At a meeting with the press,
I'd just been given the Nobel Prize
For finding happiness.
"Where do you get your great ideas?"
The news reporter said.
I looked at him and I replied,
"Off the top of my head."

I dreamt I met an Indian
In paint and feathers decked
Who thought I'd come to steal his land,
Though this was not correct,
"I come to smoke the pipe of peace,
I bring you meat and bread."
The Indian said, "I'll have a slice
Off the top of your head."

I dreamt I met Her Majesty
Making a royal visit.
I thought, "Good heavens, this is not
The nineteenth century, is it?"
The stern old Queen came up to me,
Her voice filled me with dread,
"Don't gape," she said, "and take that hat
Off the top of your head!"

I dreamt I was a monstrous thing
From drinking Jekyll's tea,
My body was alive with hair
Which grew to smother me,
Before I choked, thank God, I woke
And sat straight up in bed,
I found that all the hair had gone
Off the top of my head.

THE WOMAN I MET

I've got to tell you about this woman
I met on the train to Inverness.
It was going from Euston at eight in the evening
And leaving behind me — but here I digress
Because I must mention the storm that was growing
And blowing the snow in and coming our way.

I have to mention the state of the weather,
The weather that blew in out of the West,
It was blowing with power to check us with showers
And block us with snowfalls and cause us distress
Those terrible showers that could last for hours
And block us and shock us and cause us delay.

And did I tell you just why I was on it
This train that was going to Inverness?
I was going from Euston at eight in the evening
And leaving behind me a girl, I confess.
She'd been my lover, the wife of my brother
And he was so angry that I couldn't stay.

Yes he was angry and so I was fleeing
By sleeper to Scotland, to Inverness,
He was not far behind me and if he should find me
I feared he would kill me without much finesse;
If the storm held us and stopped us from going
Then sure he would catch me and I would be clay.

The time for leaving was almost upon us
I saw on the platform a face full of stress
But it wasn't snowing, oh would we be going?
A whistle was blowing, oh what a mess!
Then just as he saw me the train started moving
I knew he was losing as we pulled away.

I left behind me this man with a mission
I left him behind for Inverness,
I was out of his marriage and safe in my carriage
And how it was ending was anyone's guess.
Then just as I turned round, was going to sit down,
I met this woman who travelled in grey...

APRIL NOON

In a cottage close by a cool lagoon
Lives a pretty girl called April Noon
With her younger sisters, May and June,
And she's loved by March, who's a tall dragoon
With a waxed moustache and a smart platoon
Dressed in silver braids on a dark maroon.

But April wants to marry Augustus
A penniless poet who loves her just as
Much as she loves him. But March
Has money, March has charm and March
Comes after April, which is wrong.
Will she be dazzled by his bold élan?

Augustus won't give up without a fight.
His rival's tall and he is very slight
(His rival's dim and he is very bright).
He draws himself right up to his full height
And on his toes he's nimble and he's light –
Whoever said that might is always right?

The fight's soon over with Augustus hurt:
A bleeding nose, he's lying in the dirt
But April's furious, sends the proud March packing:
Has he no sense, his brainpower sadly lacking?
She bathes her lover's wounds, he is her lord
March should have known what's mightier than the
                                                    sword.

On an August day in a balmy afternoon
When the band assembled – violin, flute, bassoon –
They soon struck up that most appropriate tune.
Then April wed her poet: they left in a balloon.
On Capri's isle they'll spend their honeymoon
And, not long after, March will follow June.

and *Land of Hope and Glory* on the radio
England at its apogee, the Edwardian Age
and what more English than Sir Edward Elgar,
luxuriant moustache, aristocratic nose
high collars, tailored suits, confident smile.

But underneath, the shop-keeper's son, self-taught,
a Catholic in a Church of England world
giving piano lessons to the well-to-do,
at forty struggling to be known
believing in himself, yet often on the point
of giving up.

His wife Alice and friend Jaeger
never doubted, gave him confidence
to persevere and write *Enigma*.

Now who can hear that rich orchestration,
the swinging tunes and sweeping violins
without seeing the English countryside he loved
the Malvern Hills, the Vale of Evesham?

Or who can hear the agonised and tearing chords
of his tortured cello concerto
without sensing the man within

or meditating on the death
of that Edwardian dream
in the trenches of the Somme
the choking hell of gas at Ypres
the gangrene feet
the withered roses
of Picardy.

THE ROAD TO CAHERCIVEEN

In Dublin I experience the Easter rising,
hear the bold, humane and reasoned Declaration,
witness the pounding shells, the shattered GPO
the prisoners, the executions afterwards,
see blood on the stones of Kilmainham Gaol
as if I'd been there,
and I observe six more years of pain
before the Free State's born.

But not the Republic. "I am surprised to find
how much independence the Treaty gives
the Free State," says De Valera,
not then, but ten years later
when he'd read it carefully.
Then his voice joins the rising anger
at this bastard birth, whose bloody after-birth
soon follows as the shots ring out.

Blood feeds on blood
and by the blue-green vision
of Dingle's finger across the bay
pointing St Brendan's way to America,
the emerald road from Kells runs down
to Caherciveen. There Irish soldiers
tie their Irish prisoners to landmines,
explode them with rifle fire.

When others
pick the body parts from trees
they cannot tell that all the prisoners
are not accounted for.

SEISMIC EVENTS, 1941

When Daddy Pat came home on leave
to Sydney from Rabaul
there'd been a volcanic eruption:
when we unpacked his luggage
there was pumice dust on everything.
These things were common
since the big one in 1937
and we didn't know then
how lucky he was to get out,
before the Japanese erupted in December,
engulfed Rabaul in January.
How vital timing is: fifty-three years later
that town was obliterated
by Tavurvur and Vulcan. I have the video.

IN THE WAR MUSEUM, CANBERRA

The subdued museum lighting shadows
this coal-black killer, 26 yards long
its gaping mouth and teeth
revealing two torpedo tubes
with six propeller blades astern,
the only other 'armament' a heavy
scuttling charge.

So much space
given to these agents of death
and the motor and its shaft
it's hard to believe
two men were squeezed inside
this killing tube
five foot diameter at most.

1942. Three midget submarines
released from the parent
into the inky hostile night,
six men sent to find their way
past the Heads to targets
deep in the throat of Sydney harbour.

They knew they had too little fuel
to find retreating homes.
They knew they were too slow
to escape pursuers.
Did their funereal and claustrophobic craft
seem like coffins on a final journey?

The first crew
entangled in defensive nets
fired the scuttling charge,
destroying ship and selves.

The second
discharged their fish of death
missed the target cruiser
hit a converted ferry
killed twenty-one
were harried and destroyed.

The third
felt the depth charge blasts
that sent them to the bottom
of Taylors Bay.

In true Japanese fashion
they committed suicide
as they lay there in their tomb
its engine still running.

EXPERIENCING DEATH

We knew about danger and death;
it was all around us and daily
in newsreels Japs were flushed from foxholes
with flame-throwers or crashed their Zeros
into the bridges of warships.
The papers had a photograph,
a Japanese officer
beheading a kneeling Aussie soldier,
bare-chested and bound,
blood spurting from his neck

But the war didn't quite reach *us*,
not even on the night a submarine shelled Sydney
leaving a crater in the road
next to the one Daddy Pat and Mabsie
were living in: my grandparents,
but almost parents to me.

The front line moved further away
as the war turned and soon
Mother and I were on a troopship
heading for England,
our convoy accepting the surrender
of a German U-boat
while we wondered what might have been
if the war hadn't ended.

England and peace.
A different life,
my grandparents out of sight
and for the moment out of mind
far away in Sydney.

Then Mother's serious face
and news:
Daddy Pat was dead.
A heart attack.

And I'd never, never see him again.

.

HIROSHIMA

Imagine you must choose :
to end the war, you must either
capture the islands of Japan
one by one at cost of millions
dead, conventionally maimed,
or stop it all with just one bomb.

Imagine a world that could take the bomb
seriously, without seeing destruction
and its aftermath.

Imagine your disbelief
when Emperor and cabinet
refuse surrender
until you drop another one on Nagasaki.

Today grandchildren of the Knights of the Bushido
have hijacked the moral high ground
by rightly never letting us forget;
forgetting themselves the code of no surrender
practised by their grandfathers,
so thousands died each time
an island was recaptured from them.

The dead of
Talagi, Guadalcanal and Bougainville,
Saidor, Majuro, Kwajalein,
Eniwetok, Saipan, Guam,
Sansapur, Ulithi, Morotai,
Leyte, Manila and Luzon,
Iwo Jima, Mindanao
and all the rest :
we grieve for you.

In Okinawa, a quarter million died
before Mitsuri Ushijama chose
the ritual disembowelment of hara-kiri
rather than the shame of surrender.

THE CAPTAIN'S STORY

I
1996

Poet as tourist. Visits Villa Taranto,
Lake Maggiore, marvels at the story
of a Scottish Captain, owner of the villa,
creator of its multi-floral famous water garden.
World War Two approaching, he leaves
his garden with his gardeners
goes off to fight against their country,
but they look after it just the same, keep it safe
till his return. In gratitude
he wills it to the Italian nation.

II
2008

Poet as researcher. The world-
wide web at his command. Slowly,
hit by precious hit, he unravels
this shimmering fairy tale. In 1939,
aged 56, the Captain removes his family
to Australia, having done this deal:
He will give his villa and his garden
to the State, now, on this condition –
that it remains his private residence.
He leaves his friend and lawyer,
Cappelletto, in control and sails away.

III
1852-1910

Poet as family historian.
Why Australia? Because the Captain's father
made his fortune there: first exporter
of UK frozen meats and butter,
then owner of Australian shipping,

husband of mining millionaire's daughter,
Director of Companies, MP for Melbourne.
Defeated in elections in '04
he went off in a huff, bought a pile
in Scotland, got his son
to help him with the garden.

IV
1893

Poet gets a surprise. Captain's father,
Sir (Walter) Malcolm Donald McEacharn,
sensing chances in the shipping trade
opens passenger and cargo traffic to the west
with his new *Cloncurry, New Guinea, Coolgardie*
and *Kalgoorie* ships, carries the poet's grandfather
to make his fortune and to find his bride.
The poet's father's born, Coolgardie, 1904.

V
epilogue

Poet reflects. But, hey, this story is not mine
so what about the Captain, Neil McEacharn?
He survived the war, returned to Italy
and his garden in all its glory,
opened it to the public, 1952,
died in '64, loved by the Italian nation.

SONGS

Every day, background music on the radio
unnoticed,
but suddenly they're playing
You Belong To Me
and Jo Stafford's voice slices through the years
to take me back to one place, one time,
Nienburg on the Weser, 1953
officers of the British Army of the Rhine
occupying what had been
the best hotel in town,
a stack of records, all shellac
and young 'Pipe', fated not to survive
the coming Suez Crisis
playing this one over and over.

ALDEBURGH, MARCH 2006

The spick-and-span, new-as-paint High Street prepares
for summer. Scaffolders bristle, cement mixers churn,
tilers clamber on roofs, decorators have rooms to them
                                                    selves.
Boutiques and temples of interior décor sparkle
dreams of gracious modern living. Estate agents
flicker into life with out-of-season blandishments.
Restaurants await customers. Amber gleams
in the museum window. The Tourist Centre's glad
of any visitor, offers last year's leaflet.
This is a town waiting for the music to happen,
for the life-support festivals, the transfusion
of the literati glitterati, the artists' illusions of still life.

But we're just a building's thickness away
from the wide-angle, flat-horizoned sea
and it's this commercial barricade that's sheltering us
from the cold, grey wind cutting past the lifeboat house
and up the alley. Out there, the stony, fish-eyed sea
charges in to the sloping beach, its brown breakers
bearing evidence of its intentions and abilities.
A few scattered boats lie propped among the stones
not offering to fish today. As far as eyes can see
no boat defies the waters and no gull the wind.

Things hang in the balance. Faith is tested.
Will Aldeburgh repeat its annual resurrection
or winds roll up the beach and waves burst through
to douse the limelight, forever drown the illusion?

PRIEST'S COVE, CAPE CORNWALL

A grey, desultory sort of day. Far off,
mist hazes the landscape, converting
rocks and sea and sun to monochrome.

Lined with dry stone walls, long since
filled in with mud and moss and flat
creeping plants, a lane meanders to the sea.

Boats are all beached, but add some colour
to the work a cloth-capped artist makes
seated on an overhanging rock.

There is much to paint:

    Translucent turquoise waves
    breaking into white foam.

    The emerald velvet backdrop of creepers
    curtaining walls and cliff,
    ending as carpet on the roof
    of a seamen's hut.

    The orange floats that glow beside it.

    The red bucket and yellow T-shirts
    of two shrimping boys netting rock pools.

    A man throwing a stick
    for his three-legged mongrel sheepdog
    who runs and runs and runs
    defying his incapacity.

Waves carelessly caress the shore.
The boys put up their nets, prepare to go.
Man and dog have gone over the hill.
The artist paints on, the mist closes in.

SUNSET AT SALCOMBE

The sun throws shadows of the hill behind
far into the estuary, but lingers on the other shore
picking out amber sand, rows of neat blue boats
pushed high up the beach against the possibility
of storm, and a white house with blue shutters.
At its anchorage, a yacht is being secured for the night.
A bird flies low along the estuary towards the sea.
A dark bird, following the shoreline,
going home. I try to name it, in an idle way,
and suddenly I notice that it's blue.
I fix it, testing its blueness with each beat
until it disappears. Pondering this
I see another bird and it looks blue
and others, dipping in the shadow of our hill,
are blue and blue and blue as lights come on
tracing a pathway from yacht to house
and on up the far hillside into the luminous azure
of the darkening sky, to the first stars and all
the vast blueness of the universe beyond.

THE STONE POLISHERS

or

How they brought the Good Water from Uzés to Nîmes

They come in their thousands, shoes
polishing the hard white rock to smoothness,
to admire the grandeur of the vision and the execution
and find a scale against which to measure
the worth of water to a Roman
settling in a dry foreign land.

There's no shortage of evidence:
an aqueduct bored and channelled 31 miles around
from source to city only 7 miles away;
20 miles of tunnels;
a bridge unsurpassed in three-tiered beauty[1]
needing 1,000 men and slaves, 14 years
and 50,000 tons of stone.

Not the work of faint hearts or squabbling committees
but men of vision and of skill, who believed
in the permanence of what they did, and knew
the value of plentiful clean water to the city of Nemausus
that Augustus built in Gallia Narbonensis.

[1] Le Pont du Gard, Provence

THE BALLAD OF *TSAR KOLOKOL*

They said he was the greatest
The world had ever known
His voice boomed out like thunder
Across the Russian scene,
From Kholm to Golovino
And Plavsk they heard his call
In fields and sheds they bowed their heads
To big *Tsar Kolokol*.

They bore him to the Kremlin
Supported on a throne
Drawn by scores of horses
In glory all his own,
They took him to the tallest tower
And hoisted him up well
So all could see the majesty
Of big *Tsar Kolokol*.

The ropes were made of strongest hemp
The blocks were made of teak
The beams were hewn in Kazakhstan
From trunks of stoutest oak,
In spite of these precautions
Just how no man can tell
From such a height with all his might
Fell big *Tsar Kolokol*.

He crashed right through the scaffold
And hurtled to the ground
The fall of that colossus
Was heard for miles around,
He lay there cracked and broken
They left him where he fell
And to this year they do not dare
To move *Tsar Kolokol*[1].

---

[1] *Tsar Kolokol*, (King of Bells) is the largest bell in the world, weighs 200 tons and was made in the 18th century

DRUNK WITH WORDS

To boldly go where no man went before
To lightly fight and never call it war

To keenly seek a blessing from the gods
To lonely hope no matter what the odds

To calmly palm three aces in your hand
To gamely claim "full house" in accents bland

To thinly win by cheating at the bar
To meanly keep your pennies in a jar

To glibly split the infinitive from the 'to'
To tartly part the stocking from the shoe

To glumly love and never feel the pain
To barely wear and never mind the rain

To glowly boast that you can drink the most
To glassly raise for yet another toast

To ginly soak amongst the dregs and drogs
To slewly slosh and flounder in the bogs

To groanly gloze and drimly piss the nigh
To utter mutter, splutter throatly dry

To hubble bubble gluggle lovel fizz
To muzzle nuzzle slozzle zizzle zizzzzz...

TONY, THE GREAT REFORMER

1997

For eighteen years I've known it must be done.
The House of Lords, a Tory Old Boys' club
Must be reformed at once and now we've won

I have the power: the Tories' race is run.
I'll trim their lordships' veto like a shrub;
For eighteen years I've known it must be done.

So long we've waited, now we'll have some fun –
They'll have to hold their meetings in a pub –
It shall reform at once, now that we've won!

A detailed plan? You know that I have none
So how to do it, surely there's the rub.
For eighteen years I've known it must be done.

I've said we'll do it – ideas anyone?
It can't survive; this Tory Old Boys' hub
I will reform at once now that we've won.

I want this story well and truly spun,
My great idea: go out and thump the tub!
For eighteen years I've known it must be done:
I'll sack some peers to show them that we've won.

HISTORY IN HAIKU

Bevan's legacy:
sixty years of improving
the nation's fitness.

So celebrate our
progress to obesity
and youth's drunkenness,

better hospitals –
three hundred thousand beds less
a million more waiting[1].

Let us admit our
diamond jubilee toast's a
bitter Beveridge.

[1] *The Week*, 23rd August, 2008

INVERSION

Driven out of doors
By today's No Smoking laws
Teachers smoke instead
Behind the bicycle shed
Hope not to get caught
By pupils they've just taught.

BEFORE YOUR VERY EYES

Start with solid gold and silver

Convert into coins

Debase the metals

Replace with paper promises

Write your own

Wave your plastic wand

Conjure monthly evasions

Store in accounts

Figures on a page

Images on a screen

Virtual money

Invisible

Unreal

Gone.

ROCKET

Take a spill from Guy Fawkes' bonfire
light the blue touch paper and – woosh! –
it's away, your rocket. *We have lift-off,*
says NASA, and it goes on and on
breaks the bonds of earth and into space,
picking up rocket speed now, making for
the far confines of our solar system,
if there are any.

But alas, you'll be dead by the time it gets there
as will our civilization
and several others yet to come,
if there are any,
and its so vast, cold, empty, soundless
way out there in the universe
and your rocket is just a piece of debris
and Fawkes a forgotten name
in a book never written.

COMING – OR GOING?

The best lack all conviction. W B Yeats

A prophet has come out of the west.
The hunger of the people is aroused.

The bees are preoccupied with their own buzzing
and do not hear. Where is the hooded keeper
with the smoke? He is only concerned
with not getting stung. Good men do nothing.

They go to football or the counting house
or the superstore. They furnish their houses
with things they do not need. They fret
over lost mirages. Meanwhile

the pitcher cannot go to the well
because the well is dry. Hawks take over nests.
Birds are not building, but fly about listlessly.
There is thunder in the air and much talk
of change. The atmosphere is sullen.

Is the storm about to break or subside
in the usual way?
The buzzing is incessant.
Smoke drifts everywhere.
The prophet is far away.

IN SWITZERLAND

The sun streams in to white washed walls
onto your eager face, as the gowned
and aproned figure neither of us really knows
hands the equipment to your weak and fumbling fingers;
you grasp it so urgently that I have to intervene
and make my final peace,
not with the pale, shrunken
almost stationary wraith you have become,
so helpless and reduced,
not out of pity or love or satisfaction
that you are about to achieve your end,
but out of hot, burning rage
eating like acid into my cheeks
for the handsome, gentle, hero-worshipped
teenage brother that I lost
so many years ago.

PREVENTABLE

Murder seems too mild a word for it
the repeated beating
torture
and starvation
of toddlers
until they die,
preventable deaths
not prevented
at missed opportunity
after missed opportunity,
repeatable deaths
repeated again and again and again:
Victoria Climbié,
Danielle Reid,
Khyra Ishaq
and Baby P
and Baby Q, R, S and T
while hands are wrung
and lessons 'learned'
and systems overhauled.

Can we not hear the screams?
Feel the blows?
Smell the burns?

And will we first
run out
of letters
or excuses?

MURDER

If there must be murder
let it be by Miss Scarlet
with a Candlestick in the Conservatory.
In this world
Dr Black, our dark and devious host,
is always the victim
and murder can only be committed
with six implements:
the coward's weapon
poison is not allowed.

This is a world of grand houses
with nine ground floor rooms
including a Ball Room
where Mrs Peacock preens
and a Billiard Room
where Colonel Mustard miscues
and Mrs White is spotless.

You play Poirot or Miss Marple
asking inspired questions
(like, "Why does the Revolver
have no revolving parts?")
until at last,
with all gathered together
in the same room,
the murderer is unmasked
and all is revealed
in a sealed envelope.

WALKING TO KINGS COPPICE FARM

October

The sun is warm, but doesn't burn.
The breeze is cool, but doesn't freeze.
This is weather to enjoy forever.

No crops flank the path, but
far as eye can see, the earth
is burnt sienna, harrowed to fine tilth
littered with rounded stones and jagged flints.

No birds in sight
and nothing moves but you, alone
in all this space, who have become
its only spectacle, watched
by low white houses peering
into the valley. In the distance
a whit-whit-whit and chup-chup-chup
of turkeys fattening in the orchard.

Beside the path a few decapitated
plants, all that survive
the onslaught of machinery.
You turn around, look back against the sun
and are aware a faint green tinge
has spread across the land. Not weeds
or winter wheat, but kale
ploughed in and disced to pieces,
a sacrificial offering to tomorrow.

February

The sky scowls and the wind charges
up the valley, fixed bayonets piercing
cracks in body armour. Grass
bends to the ground. Clay
bonds to soles like chewing gum. The farm,
still out of sight, seems miles away.
Was it wise to take this path?
Can't be helped. Head down, one foot
in front of the other. Leaning into it.

Bend comes and farm's visible,
its bare hedge of sharp spikes
and welcoming barred metal gate.
A sudden squall brings
full frontal attack of ice missiles
and then a lull. Cease fire? Look !
Suddenly an emissary in a white vest
running towards you – to offer a truce?
Just as quickly he's past, eyes averted
intent on personal salvation of some sort.

There's nothing for it but to battle on
hoping there'll be snowdrops in the lane.

April

Cambridge blue sky,
powder-puff clouds still as kestrels.
A cool breeze gentles your face.
February's 'grass' now hints at wheat
marching in line up both slopes,
atop which straw coats still protect
tender plantlings by the hedge.
Smudges of white and pink
dust trees here and there.
Sun paints lawns, makes houses smile.
No one's about.

It's thirsty work and at the farm
you branch off up the hill
past empty turkey fields and sheds.
Trees and houses on your right
duck below the rim. Yaffles
express their irritation
over some unseen intruder.

You're at the top now, disappear
through V-shaped stile
into the tangly, mired paths
that lead to ale.

August

The path is soft with straw. Bow waves
of ground rise on either side. Ahead
lies every shade of gold and amber
that the world possesses
curving to the blue horizon.
A bee buzzes round your feet
and where the path bends out of view
four rooks eye you,
decide that there is time,
pursue their business.

On the slope's peak, a stand
of half a dozen trees keeps lookout.
Suddenly a pigeon breaks cover,
flaps away.   The rooks confer.
One by one they lift, part,
then wheel and come together
to reconvene their coven
on some other ground.

The sun sinks behind low clouds.
The air is warm, the breeze cooling.
All around you is a world of calm.
Taste the air.   Feel the silence.

AN ENGLISH WINTER'S TALE
With thanks to Louis MacNeice

Oh dear, oh dear, it snowed last night
The city streets are cloaked in white
At least three inches of the stuff
Have blocked the roads, it's quite enough.

So it's no go to school today, it's no go to the office
The wrong stuff's on the lines today and the buses are all in the
garage.

The Council has run out of grit
They never thought it would come to it
The teachers can't get in today
The children have gone off to play.

So it's no go the motorway, it's no go the by-pass
My bike is under a load of hay and I've lost my uncle's eyeglass.

The snow plough's stuck at the Council tip
Behind ten tanks and a rusty ship
They've quite forgotten where it lurks
Or even how the damn thing works.

So it's no go the shovels and spades, it's no go brawn and braces
We've all downed tools and we're off to watch the local downhill
races.

It's not that we really want to shirk
It just isn't healthy or safe to work
It's not that the roads are really icy
But we're not taking risks when the odds are dicey.

So it's no go production quotas, it's no go the targets
Dad's gone down to the *Rose and Crown* and the kids have gone to
Margate

THE SECOND DAY

Yesterday white covered all, empowering youth
with riots of energy.
Today ice constrains the old, infirm, indoors.

The sun bursts brilliantly for a moment
blinding with whiteness.
Flakes whirl suddenly around, are driven away
in a flurry of casual wind.

Yesterday's flock of redwings in the orchard,
glad of February apples, are gone.

In the shadowed garden
A Witch Hazel is transformed
into a Cotton Wool Tree.
There are traysful of birds
and a pigeon sits patiently
on a white cushion.

Where it can reach,
a sunbrush paints grey into white.

The day hangs in the balance
between frozen caution and enabling warmth.

If this is a thaw, it's mighty slow.
The sun gives up, goes home.
A car creeps like a snail, down the lane.

WILD SEEDS

They come from nowhere
lodge in crevices, resist
all attempts to eject them,
irritate, puzzle, confuse
but you keep coming back
water them a little
against your inclinations
and they take root, grow
force themselves to the forefront
so that you give them space
removing others.
Now they're quite big, demanding
need tending, shaping, feeding,
demand time, more time
but you can't let go,
push them forward
talk about them constantly
exhibit them, win attention,
keep throwing others out of bed
until there's only this one
huge, dominant, commanding
all your waking hours.

PLANTS

His quick eyes assess the situation.
Nothing seems to be available
but on his cue he's down
lining things up.
There's brief contact –
a glancing angle –
that double click
as one red stays still
and the other rolls
across the green baize
into the left-hand pocket.

Next day, the silverware
checked in with his baggage,
he's walking across the concourse
pleased with his night's work,
doesn't see the man approaching
at an oblique angle,
accepts the collision with good grace
is quite unaware
of the small round packet
nestling in the left pocket
of his green velvet jacket.

RITE OF PASSAGE

The moon goes round the earth in an ellipse
and in its time makes many monthly trips,
the earth and moon and sun are passing ships
which now and then align: moon shadow clips
the earth and where it does, day slowly slips
from sight. Life stops. An eerie darkness grips
wild living things with fear and each heart skips
a beat. The sun's rim flares with fiery whips
and throats go dry as some with hollow quips
dismiss their fears with science on their lips
as in their souls they fear apocalypse.
They wait and watch: the perspiration drips.
Day fights with night and then the balance tips
as colours glow: the end of the eclipse.

CREATION

I'm talking about the maker
of all sub-atomic particles
and a universe so large
we don't know where it ends
or if it has an end;
the giver of life to the fly's eye,
whale's tail, lyre bird and worm;
creator of a system so complex
that it evolved itself once set in motion.
Does this being need our worship,
care whether we believe in him
or not? A jealous God?
From Proxima Centauri
there's no proof that we exist.
How long's our span in all eternity?
In His own image, we say, being blind,
when we've created Him so like our own.

ADVICE TO PILGRIMS

7th July 2005

Bid farewell to your loved ones
with a light heart.

Leave early in the morning
for you have far to travel.

Carry a copy of the Holy Book
for meditation.

Take no more money than is sufficient
for the completion of your journey.

Take nothing with you
that you do not need.

Bear your burden
on your back.

Travel with someone
who shares your purpose;
your task will seem easier.

Talk no more than is necessary
but keep your mind focussed
on the reason for your journey.

If doubts assail you, think of the rewards
when you reach your journey's end.

When you arrive
do what you have come to do
at the place and time appointed
for the uplifting of your immortal soul.

VIGIL

In the hollows of the night I search for you
my first born, that I might fill
this childless void beyond my comprehension.

Where are you?
Did you find that paradise
that those who'd never seen it promised you?

And did you meet the wandering spirits
of the unbelievers who went with you
in that moment you abandoned me?

And did they forgive you? Or are you
suffering the torments of their hell,
or worse, are you nowhere?

Tell me, my beloved son,
tell me my emptiness is not in vain
as in the hollows of the night, I search for you.

DISCRIMINATION

Do not speak ill of my beliefs

Do not speak ill of me

Do not speak of your beliefs

Do not speak

Believe me

Share my beliefs

Do not stop sharing my beliefs

There is no turning back

once you have embraced my faith

WHAT DID YOU DO IN THE WAR, FATHER?

I trained our gallant soldiers
taught them how to fight
for God and Country.

But what else did you do in the war, Father?

I gave our soldiers belief.
I stiffened their resolve.
I made stirring speeches.

And what about the fighting, Father?

I put our troops through their paces
showed them exactly what to do
explained how they could destroy the enemy.

Tell me how they did it, Father.

They filled barrows with hidden explosives
positioned them close to the enemy.
Then they were blown up.

These troops were your bravest, Father?

Yes. Young boys were best,
caused least suspicion, died like men
when I pressed the button.

THE SICILIAN DEFENCE

Pawn to Queen's Bishop four
rejects the idea that the game must be played
on White's terms. Black calls the tune,
offers White nothing but struggle.
Learn the opening
in all its variations
and you can put off thinking
for ages.

Or join that other black Sicilian defence
and it's just the same: obey the code
and life simplifies, thinking can be postponed.
Or obey the codes of our peers,
gang, Party, Nation, Church or Mosque
and you have nothing to worry about.

There's this great feeling of belonging,
a pattern of life which smoothes the way ahead
removes difficult decisions
lets us get on with things, confident
in our strength and our defences.

POETIC LICENCE

Now then, sir,
please switch your engine off.
I've been watching you
erratic steering
for the last half mile
at least.
Using a mobile phone, were we?

Writing a poem. With a pen.
On paper. One hand on the wheel.
In a hurry to get it down.
Why didn't you stop?

Collecting a poet
from the station.
He was late.
So will you be, sir.

"Not - in control - of your
poem …while driving a vehicle …"
Just breathe into this, please sir.

A WILD, FLOWERY TALE

In April, the poet's narcissus blows
his own trumpet, but by May
he looks for blue-eyed Mary in the woods
and jack-go-to-bed-at-noon soon follows.
He should be in clover, but alas
spends too many scented hours
in another lady's bedstraw.
Now winds the viper's bugloss
and wags the adderstongue.
"Mind your own business" shouts
from banks and walls
but can this salsify her?
Oh, wormwood, wormwood and bittersweet!
He suffers in tormentil, condemned
to pay her agrimony. What's left to him?
Only selfheal, selfheal.

LARGS AFTER DARK

I knew a visitor to Largs who'd leave his digs
at dead of night and hasten to the green
so smoothly mown along the front, and there
he'd park his bike by boards and not be seen

by anyone: there was no one about.
Taking his torch, he shone it on the words
painted so neatly by the Town Clerk's scribe
in foot-high letters, black on chalk-white boards:

BURGH OF LARGS, NO FOOTBALL's what they said
and he would smile, take off his cycle clips
and roll his trousers almost to the knees.
A merry tune was humming on his lips

as from his bag he took a pumped-up ball
and kicked it hard along the sacred sward,
then dribbled left and right with many a turn
and feint; he was as happy as a lord.

And now and then he'd take a shot into
a coiffeured bush, or fiercely bang the ball
into a fence while proudly murmuring "goal!"
or beat a man, then slam it against a wall.

He couldn't keep it up, his spirit willing
but aging lungs and legs not what they were
and he'd flop down upon the Council's seat
and take his ease and breathe the Council's air.

Then with a smile he'd stow his ball away
roll down his trousers, put his clips in place
collect his bike beneath the Council's words
and pedal off, the smile still on his face.

Next morning, waking late, he'd stagger down
to breakfast, eat his porridge, bacon, toast,
thank his landlady; yes, he had slept well,
it was the air, the finest on the coast.

CROSSING IRELAND BY TRAIN, 2007

I – ON ROSSLARE STRAND

What made some pacing passengers irate
Was that the only Rosslare train was late
Communications failure was the cause
The PA stated, clutching at straws.

This was an Irish explanation
For the driver's lateness at the station
(Hung over after last night's crawl
He hadn't heard his alarm at all, at all).

II – AT LIMERICK JUNCTION

The Dublin express bound for Cork
Did not appear at Limerick station:
This led to frivolous speculation
About diversions to Dundalk.

The explanation was much more benign:
The train was late – there were *cows on the line.*

NOT MENTIONING CRICKET

Although the summer season's started
And bat on ball makes me light-hearted
And willow and I will not be parted
I don't mention the game.

I will not praise that mecca of places
For meeting familiar and famous faces
Which once was blessed by all three Graces:
I won't give its name.

I'm fired by the power, seduced by the style
The speed of the pacemen, the spinners of guile
Oh, the hits that can travel for many a mile –
But I won't fan its flame.

The hits and the heroes, the fabulous feats
The matches and catches, the flying stump treats
The facts and the figures, the sighs and the sweets –
I won't make any claim.

Some say it's boring, some say it's slow
But they are the people who never will go
To see what it offers, so how do they know?
I think it's a shame.

A MOMENT WITH MONTY

Under his black patka, his soft brown eyes
are thoughtful, rehearsing what must be done.
He twirls the ball in the fingers of his left
repeatedly spins it to his right.

Then, three short paces
breaks into a run
body, rocking back,
swings round his planted foot
rotating as the ball
snaps from his fingers,
loops,
drifts away a little.

Chanderpaul, seventy-four runs secure,
judges there's no danger, makes no move
to play it. Spin bites,
ball breaks back at speed
strikes him on the pad.

Monty's arm is up, his shout's insistent, eyes appealing.
Up goes the umpire's finger and
off goes Monty
like a fire-cracker,
a jumping jack
exploding into air,
landing and springing off again
in new surprise directions.

The team catch fire with him,
ignition spreads from man to man
crosses the long space to the boundary
leaps the fence
and lights the crowd,
spreads like a brush fire

so that,
when the moment comes
off its high point,
as it must,
there's a buzz everywhere
and people
returning to their seats
can feel the warmth
of sharing
a moment with Monty.

THINGS

Walking round Cliveden again
we watch children rolling like wayward logs
down the slope to the Parterre,
say how much they love doing it
but then they always did
"and always will," you add,

but I think of what's changed
over the years, of the poor quality
of the grass now – starved, thin –
the plank-protected staircase balustrade
Canning's Oak horizontal,
and wonder if they always will.

Things go on, apparently the same
and we think they will always be the same
but they die, crumble, fail
have to be replaced
by things which may be just as good
but different

and the grandchildren's memories
are not the same as the grandparents'
who are saddened by what is lost,
while the grandchildren
are happily harvesting their sepia-tinted memories,
which one day
they will want to share
with their children and grandchildren
even if, by then
things are not the same.

THE BOY

I'm looking through a window of a school,
a boarding school. A boy is sitting at a desk
while others play or read,
but he seems unaware of them
drawing his semi-circles, parallel lines.
The glass is smudged, but the shape seems familiar.
It's a miniature athletics track.
He rolls the dice

and suddenly it's a summer's day
and there they are, the great Arthur Wint,
Herb McKinley, Mal Whitfield
and an overflowing crowd.
Maureen Gardner skims hurdles like a bird
but Fanny Blankers-Koen catches her,
hits the final barrier.
They breast the tape together
and the British crowd goes wild.
But it's Fanny's second gold and the whole sky
is golden and the silver world revolves
to a kaleidoscope of sounds
and the war and rationing
are in a distant age.

The boy smiles as he calculates
winning times by his own method,
writes down the order of finishing,
presents the medals,
closes the book.

RACING CERTAINTY

For Amy ElizabethTurner[1]

Our Melbourne Cup is over.
The runners and the riders have paraded
shown their form, run their races
and are gone.

Makybe Diva[2] has made history
and thousands richer

but we're enriched by one small diva
who came from nowhere to astonish us.
We have our money on her and the whole stable
who made her possible,
attend her needs,
put her through her paces,
give her fields to run in. She's a winner.

I will put my shirt on it.

[1] Born in Melbourne, 24 March 2005, visited 10 October – 2 November 2005
[2] On 1 November 2005, won Australia's premier horse race for the third successive year

DOWN THE GARDEN

This is the grass which children couldn't harm
with all their games and here a willow wept
its golden tears, then built the children's den,
and here borders smiled tulips, pinks
and nodding aquilegia, so vulnerable to balls,
and mother sighed.

The willow tree has gone, and we progress down
the garden, past the laurel hedge, to beds
where fruit is over and the garden
narrows: on one side, fleeting
scented sweet viburnum,
and on the other, prickling
holly hedge, impenetrable.
Past the well-meaning
pittosporum and the
compost heaps,
it closes to
a point.

    Beyond that
     stood a single tree,
it's said, promising Bramleys
or delicious eaters. The holly's
    now so high, so dense
      we cannot see
       what lies
       beyond,
        if
       anything.

LEMON THYME

In winter, she shrinks into the soil
hoping not to be noticed
until her strength returns.
And when the world revives,
warms with promise of heady days
she steals from her bed, sends out
green scouts, battalions of spears,
while underground her burrowing armies
channel below concrete barriers,
erupt to ambush late sleepers, outnumber them
take over the place. And suddenly the lazy gardener
becomes aware of what she's done, looks crossly
at her, threatens her with a stick,
but she only smiles, accepts the beating
overpowers him with her sweet humour
and calms his mood. *Surely*, she asks,
we can do a deal about this?

BIRDS

When I was young and eager
The gardens that I knew
Had linnets, wrens and goldfinches
That carolled as they flew

The skies were full of skylarks
With mallards on the ponds
The night-song was the nightingale's
The rivers all had swans

But now that I am older
With time for fears and woes
My garden's full of magpies
and sparrowhawks and crows.

MAGPIE

You arrive as though you know you're unwelcome
land a distance from your objective
transfer weight from foot to foot
cocking your head on one side, then the other,
eyeing the occupants of the lawn.
Will the blackbird remember
your last raid on her nest?
Will the collared dove
stand up to you? Will I appear?

Then you advance in stages,
a ne'er do well uncle
looking for a soft touch.
A large piece of bread
is almost within stabbing range.
One, two – a lunge – and you have it,
flickering up and away to the bird bath,
a quick drowning, a rolling it around,
an extraction with black tweezers, then
off to your treetop refuge
like a thief who knows
the cops have been called.

Sometimes you'll beak your booty,
make a surreptitious flit to the laurel bush,
a re-emergence without bread,
with a self-satisfied
no-one-knows-my-hiding-place look
and return once more
to try your luck with the combative dove,
the nervous blackbird, the uncertain human
with the dubious motives.

TIME LAPSE

Since we have every copy of *Which?* there's ever been
we don't throw them out,
but pile them on the spare bed until another twelve are saved
then put them in the loft,
and the pile on the bed grows faster with the years
until it looks like time-lapse photography
the copies landing one on top of another in quick succession –
flip, flip, flip, flip and another year's gone –
and there seems no way of slowing the movie down
let alone freezing the frames
and you suppose it's because you're so busy
and wonder how it'd be
if you did nothing – really nothing –
like a patient lying paralysed on a bed
waiting for death, for whom you'd think
time must really drag, but it's an experiment
you hope you'll never have to try.

UNDER SIEGE

On the face of it, our curtain wall
looks intact, supplies get through
and we go about our business.
But the besiegers tunnel
into our defences, sap our strength.

They have had notable successes.
Damage to the keep
has been patched up. The postern
creaks on its hinges. A watchtower
was almost slighted.

The defenders do their best:
attacks are repulsed,
sorties bring temporary relief,
morale remains high.
But we all know
it's a matter of time.

In the end
the walls will be breached
the barbican will yield
the inner bailey will be penetrated
the donjon will be undermined
and the Constable
will surrender.

HOW TIME IS SLIPPING

The sun is waning in the evening sky
A shadow passes travelling on a wall
A coiled spring oh so carefully unwinds
And on its chain, a hanging weight must fall

A pendulum is slowing to stand still
and running water runs and runs away
A battery becomes an empty cell
A radioactive element decays

A candle waxes, burns away as gas
and metal tarnishes, goes matt, or rusts
A grub reduces wool to wool that was
A beetle bores and what was wood is dust

A rotten bough is creaking and then breaks
The sickly tree will be the first to go
A fallen apple's falling prey to beaks
And carrion flesh becomes a meal for crows

Bodies that are gross will soon be less
And ice that once was solid starts to melt
The desert sand is creeping over grass
And as we wring our hands our milk is spilt.

MIGHTIER

The sword of Damocles
is at my throat
ready at a stroke
to cut off
the flow
of words
from their home
in the left
to my pen,
render me
speechless,
left-handed
or worse.
I've felt
its power
grazing
the surface,
showing
what it can do.
Now I know
it's there
I shall be
more careful,
work even
harder
to make
words
my
best

.

THE BED I SLEPT IN

The bed I slept in as a child
is too short now. The dreams I dreamt
there long ago were much too wild
to light my later years and guide
my stumbling feet. Put them away
and with a careful stride, watching
each footfall on the uneven track,
avoid the sudden dangers of
the path. But do not quite forget
them. Still recall their momentary
brilliance and the pure delight
they gave and let those beacons shine
brightly once more, before I go
into the silence of the night.